Vaudeville & Menuet

16 Easy to Intermediate Pieces from 18th-century France, for Violin (Flute or Oboe) and Keyboard, and optional Cello (Bassoon)

16 pièces françaises du XVIIIe siècle de niveau facile à moyen pour violon (ou flûte, ou hautbois) et clavier, avec violoncelle (ou basson) facultative

16 einfache bis mittelschwere Musikstücke aus dem Frankreich des 18. Jahrhunderts, für Geige (Flöte oder Oboe) und Klavier, sowie Cello (Fagott) ad lib.

Edited by / Edition de / Herausgegeben von

Jeremy Barlow

ED 12862
ISMN M-2201-2392-4

www.schott-music.com

Mainz · London · Madrid · New York · Paris · Prague · Tokyo · Toronto

Contents / Sommaire / Inhalt

ED 12862

British Library Cataloguing-in-Publication Data.
A catalogue record for this book is available from the British Library.
ISMN M-2201-2392-4

French translation: Agnès Ausseur
German translation: Ute Corleis
Cover design: H.-J. Kropp
Music setting and page layout by Figaro
Printed in Germany S&Co.8038

Preface / Préface / Vorwort

In 18th-century France (as in other parts of Europe) a well-known tune might be used interchangeably for a song setting, a dance, or for instrumental performance. The title of this album derives from the vaudeville, a light song in which new words (often satirical) were given to an existing tune, and from the minuet, the principal ballroom dance until the waltz (and the Revolution) swept it away towards the end of the century. At a ball, the minuet was usually danced by one couple at a time in front of the assembled company, and it contrasted with the contredanse, in which several or many couples participated together (exceptionally, **7** is a combined minuet and contredanse). The music has been selected from reduced scores of operas and ballets, and from collections of dance tunes and instrumental pieces, published in Paris during the first half of the 18th century.

Players may follow the 18th-century practice of performing sequences or suites of dance movements in related keys; for example **1–3**; **4–6**; **8–9**; **7**, **10–11**; **12–13**, **16**. One might play **14** with any of the other pieces in D major or minor (**4–6**, **10–11**), and **15** with one or both of the pieces in A minor (**8–9**).

Vaudeville & Menuet forms part of the Schott series Baroque Around the World. Other volumes include *Thistle & Minuet* (Scottish baroque music, ED 12773) and *English Airs and Dances* (ED 12861).

En France, au XVIIIe siècle (comme ailleurs en Europe), un air connu pouvait servir de façon interchangeable à une chanson, une danse ou un morceau instrumental. Ce recueil emprunte son titre au vaudeville, chanson légère sur laquelle on mettait de nouvelles paroles (souvent satiriques), et au menuet, principale danse de salon jusqu'à ce que la valse (et la Révolution) ne la supplante vers la fin du siècle. Au bal, le menuet, habituellement dansé par un seul couple à la fois devant l'assemblée, s'opposait à la contredanse à laquelle participaient plusieurs couples (le n°**7** est exceptionnel en ce qu'il associe menuet et contredanse). Cette sélection a été réalisée à partir de réductions de partitions d'opéras et de ballets, ainsi que de recueils de danses et d'airs instrumentaux, tous publiés à Paris au cours de la première moitié du XVIIIe siècle.

Les interprètes pourront renouer avec la pratique en usage au XVIIIe siècle de jouer des suites de mouvements de danses dans des tonalités voisines, par exemple les pièces **1** à **3** ; **4** à **6** , **8** et **9** ; **7**, **10** à **11** ; **12** à **13**, **16**. On pourra jouer le n°**14** avec tout autre pièce en *ré* majeur ou mineur (**4** à **6**, **10** à **11**) et le n°**15** avec l'une ou les deux pièces en *la* mineur (**8** et **9**).

Vaudeville & Menuet appartient à la collection *Baroque around the World* éditée chez Schott et qui compte parmi ses autres volumes *Thistle & Minuet* (musique baroque écossaise, ED 12773) et *English Airs and Dances* (ED 12861).

Im Frankreich des 18. Jahrhunderts konnte eine wohlbekannte Melodie (genau wie in anderen Teilen Europas) austauschbar als Liedvertonung, Tanz oder für Instrumentalaufführungen benutzt werden. Der Titel dieses Bandes stammt einerseits vom Vaudeville, einem spaßhaften Lied, in dem einer bestehenden Melodie ein neuer Text (oft satirischer Art) unterlegt wurde. Andererseits stammt er vom Menuett, das der führende Tanz in den Ballsälen war, bis der Walzer (und die Revolution) es gegen Ende des Jahrhunderts weggefegt haben. Auf einem Ball wurde das Menuett normalerweise immer abwechselnd nur von einem Paar auf einmal vor der versammelten Gesellschaft getanzt. Es stand damit im Kontrast zu den Contretänzen, an denen mehrere oder sogar viele Paare teilnahmen (ausnahmsweise ist Nr. **7** eine Mischung aus Menuett und Contretanz). Die Musik wurde aus Partiturauszügen von Opern und Balletten ausgewählt, sowie aus Sammlungen mit Tanzmelodien und Instrumentalstücken, die während der ersten Hälfte des 18. Jahrhunderts in Paris veröffentlicht wurden.

Spieler können der Praxis aus dem 18. Jahrhundert folgen und Sequenzen oder Suiten mit Tanzsätzen in verwandten Tonarten aufführen, z.B. **1–3**; **4–6**; **8–9**; **7**, **10–11**; **12–13**, **16**. Stück **14** kann man mit jedem der anderen Stücke in D-Dur oder D-Moll kombinieren (**4–6**, **10–11**) und **15** mit einem oder beiden Stücken in a-Moll (**8–9**).

Vaudeville & Menuet ist Teil der Schott Reihe *Baroque around the World*. Andere Bände daraus sind *Thistle & Minuet* (schottische Barockmusik, ED 12773) und *English Airs and Dances* (ED 12861).

About the Editor

Jeremy Barlow has made a special study of popular and dance music from the 16th to 18th centuries. His many editions include *The Music of John Gay's The Beggar's Opera* (Oxford University Press) and *The Complete Country Dance Tunes from Playford's Dancing Master, 1651–c.1728* (Faber Music). Recent writings include *The Enraged Musician: Hogarth's Musical Imagery* (Ashgate) and *The Cat and the Fiddle: Images of Musical Humour from the Middle Ages to Modern Times* (Bodleian Library, Oxford).

L'éditeur

Jeremy Barlow a concentré ses recherches sur la musique populaire du XVIe au XVIIIe siècles. Ses nombreuses publications comprennent *The Music of John Gay's The Beggar's Opera* (Oxford University Press) et *The Complete Country Dance Tunes from Playford's Dancing Master, 1651–c.1728* (Faber Music). Parmi ses écrits les plus récents figurent *The Enraged Musician: Hogarth's Musical Imagery* (Ashgate) et *The Cat and the Fiddle: Images of Musical Humour from the Middle Ages to Modern Times* (Bodleian Library, Oxford).

Der Herausgeber

Jeremy Barlow hat sich besonders mit der Popularmusik des 16. bis 18. Jahrhunderts befasst. Seine vielen Ausgaben umfassen *The Music of John Gay's The Beggar's Opera* (Oxford University Press) und *The Complete Country Dance Tunes from Playford's Dancing Master, 1651–c.1728* (Faber Music). Jüngere Veröffentlichungen sind unter anderem *The Enraged Musician: Hogarth's Musical Imagery* (Ashgate) und *The Cat and the Fiddle: Images of Musical Humour from the Middle Ages to Modern Times* (Bodleian Library, Oxford).

1. March pour les matelots

Marin Marais

2. Air

Joseph Bodin de Boismortier

3. Rondeau

To be played in rondo form:
sections ABACADA in sequence

Joseph Bodin de Boismortier

C
C
D
D
D. C. al Fine

4. Brunette 'Je suis charmé d'une brune'

Michel Pinolet de Montéclair

Double (Variation)

5. Gigues 1 & 2

Michel Corette

Gigue 1

Fine

Gigue 2

6. Vaudeville

Michel Corette

7. Le Menuet à 4–6 coupé

Collected by Charles Nicolas Le Clerc

8. La chapelière

Collected by Charles Nicolas Le Clerc

9. Les Grâces et l'enjouement

Collected by Charles Nicolas Le Clerc

25
1.
2.
[♩ = 96]
1.
2.
Tambourin
29
33
38
(𝄋)
(To 𝄋 2nd time)

10. La chasse galante

Collected by Charles Nicolas Le Clerc

Vaudeville & Menuet

16 Easy to Intermediate Pieces from 18th-century France, for Violin (Flute or Oboe) and Keyboard, and optional Cello (Bassoon)

16 pièces françaises du XVIIIe siècle de niveau facile à moyen pour violon (ou flûte, ou hautbois) et clavier, avec violoncelle (ou basson) facultative

16 einfache bis mittelschwere Musikstücke aus dem Frankreich des 18. Jahrhunderts, für Geige (Flöte oder Oboe) und Klavier, sowie Cello (Fagott) ad lib.

Edited by / Edition de / Herausgegeben von
Jeremy Barlow

ED 12862
ISMN M-2201-2392-4

www.schott-music.com

Mainz · London · Madrid · New York · Paris · Prague · Tokyo · Toronto
© 2006 Schott & Co. Ltd, London

Contents / Sommaire / Inhalt

ED 12862
British Library Cataloguing-in-Publication Data.
A catalogue record for this book is available from the British Library.
ISMN M-2201-2392-4

French translation: Agnès Ausseur
German translation: Ute Corleis
Cover design: H.-J. Kropp
Music setting and page layout by Figaro
Printed in Germany S&Co.8038

1. March pour les matelots

2. Air

Violoncello (Bassoon)

3. Rondeau

To be played in rondo form:
sections ABACADA in sequence

Joseph Bodin de Boismortier

© 2006 Schott & Co. Ltd, London

4. Brunette 'Je suis charmé d'une brune'

Michel Pinolet de Montéclair

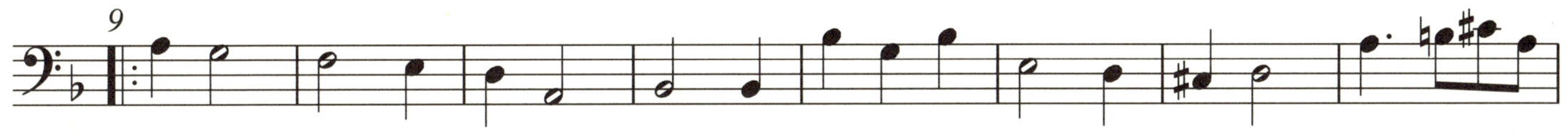

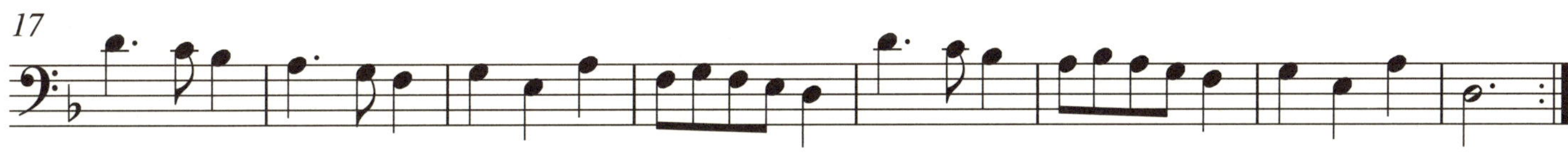

Double (Variation)

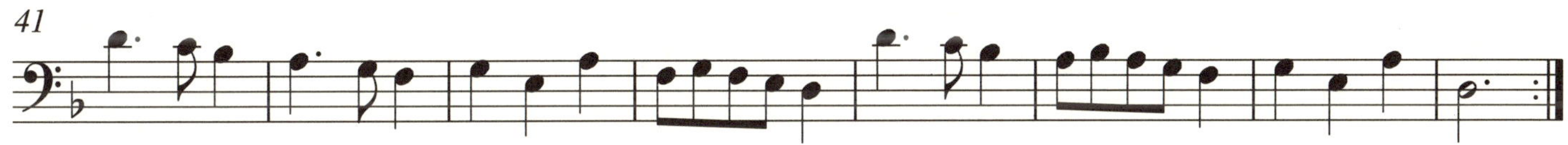

5. Gigues 1 & 2

Gigue 1

Michel Corette

[Lively 2 ♩. = 96]

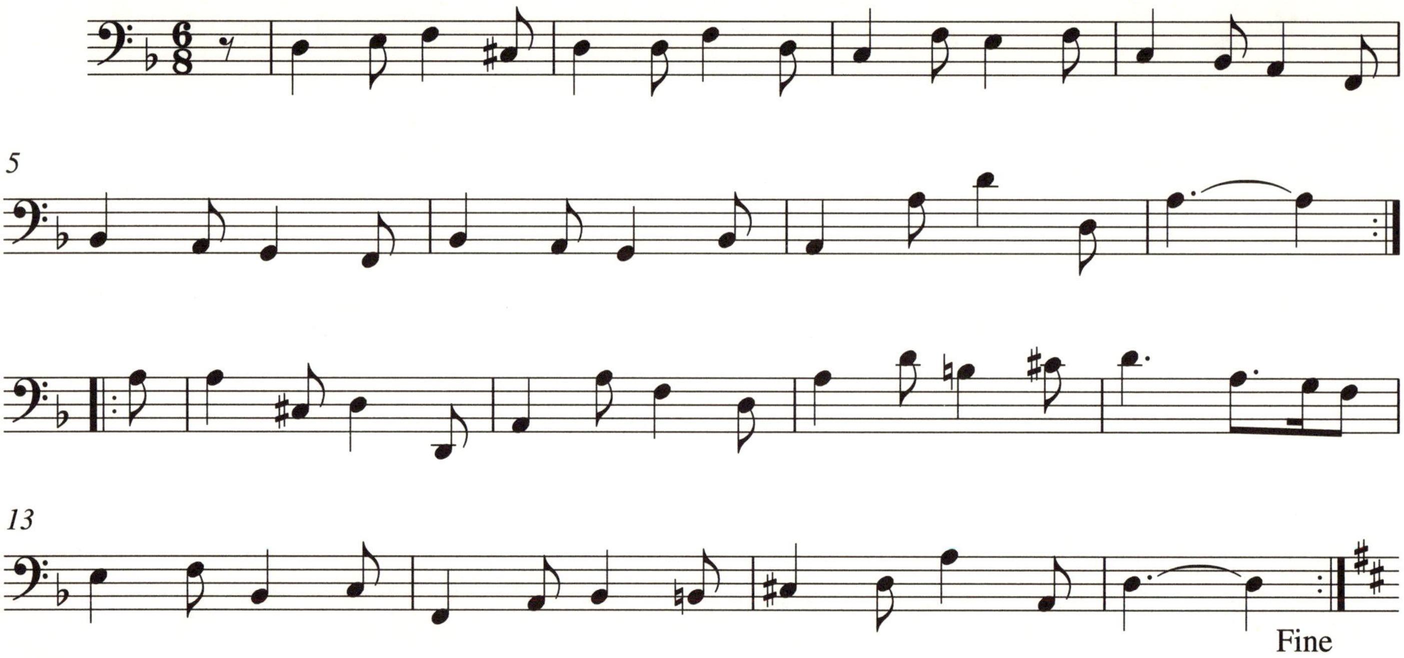

Gigue 2

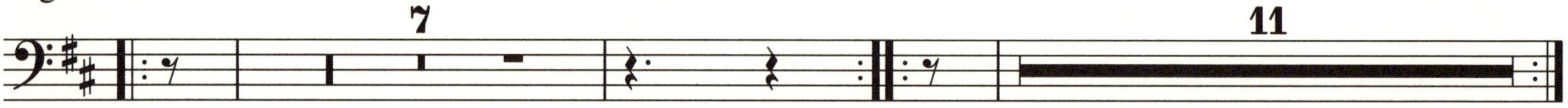

D. C. Gigue 1 al Fine

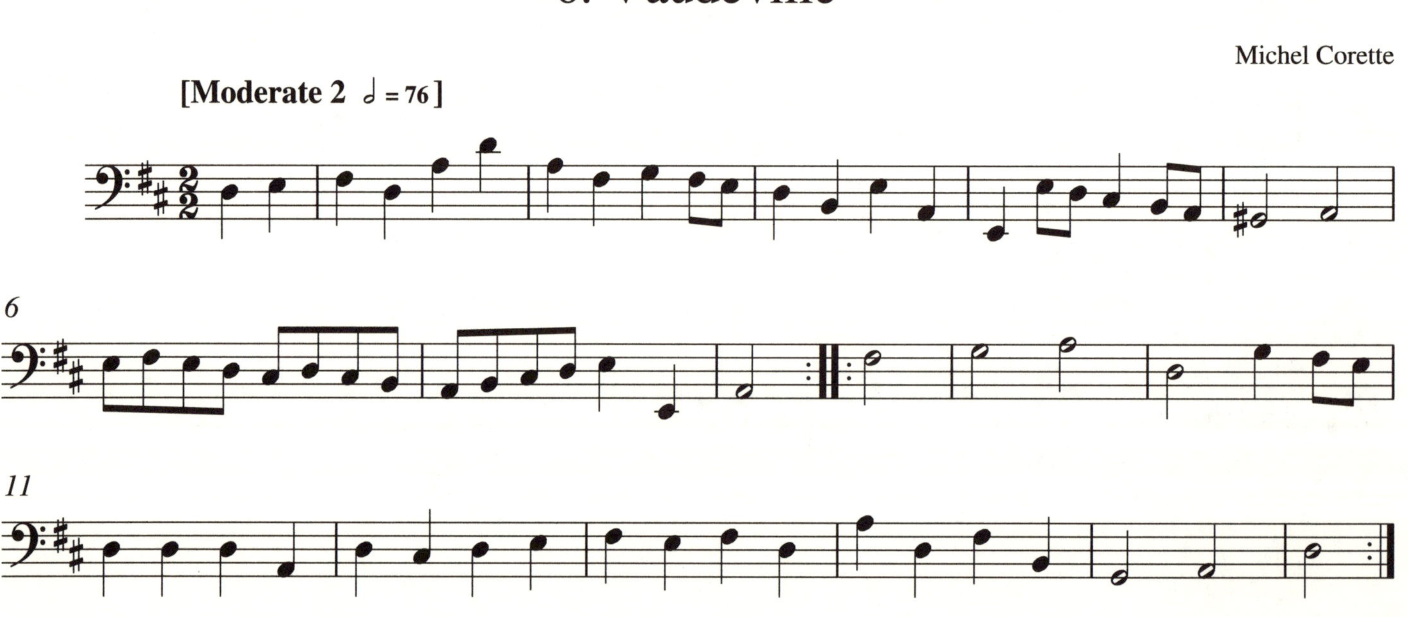

6. Vaudeville

Michel Corette

[Moderate 2 𝅗𝅥 = 76]

7. Le Menuet à 4–6 coupé

Collected by Charles Nicolas Le Clerc

8. La chapelière

Collected by Charles Nicolas Le Clerc

9. Les Grâces et l'enjouement

Collected by Charles Nicolas Le Clerc

Menuet [flowing one in a bar ♩. = 48]

© 2006 Schott & Co. Ltd, London

10. La chasse galante

Collected by Charles Nicolas Le Clerc

[Lively 2 ♩ = 96]

© 2006 Schott & Co. Ltd, London

11. Gavotte and Air

Pierre de Lagarde

12. Branle de Metz

Collected by Leclerc

[Steady 2 𝅗𝅥. = 84]

13. Airs 1 & 2

Jean Joseph de Mondonville

Air 1

Léger [♩ = 96]

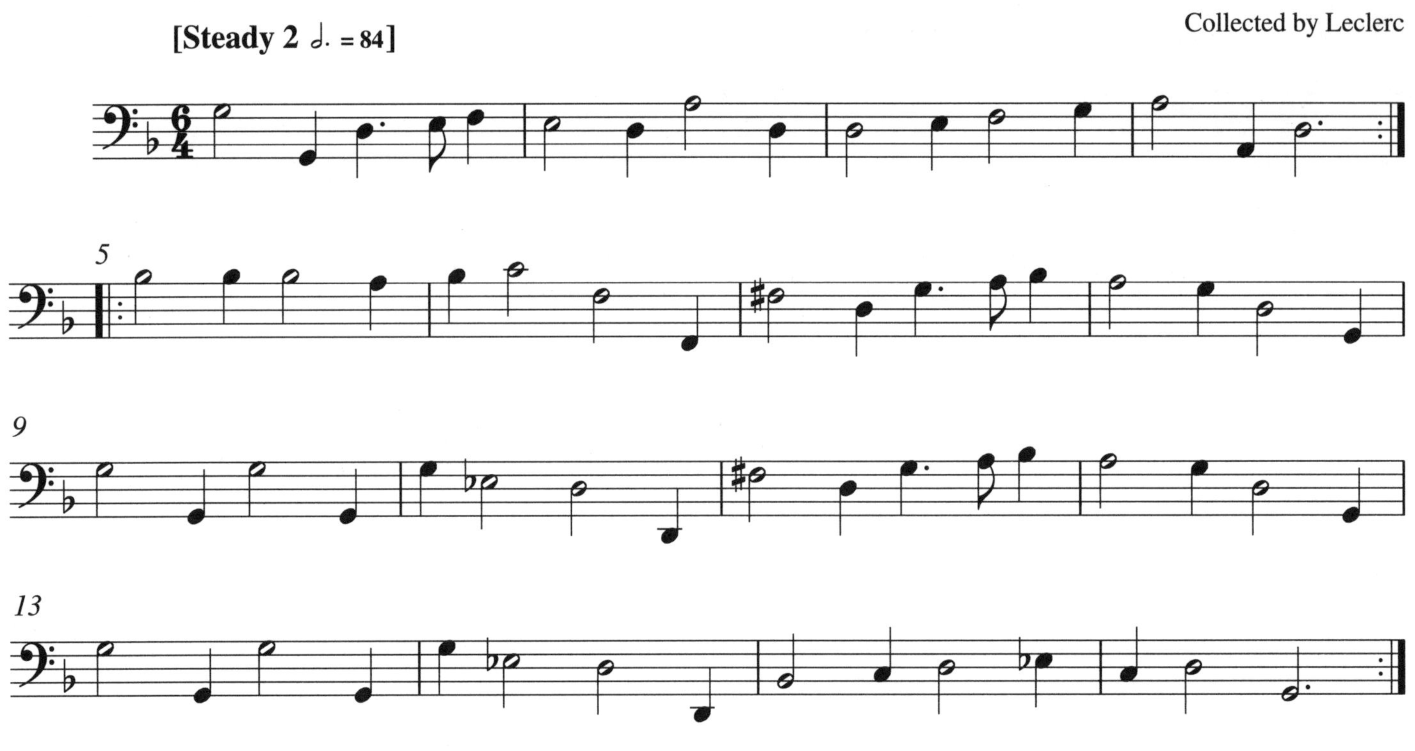

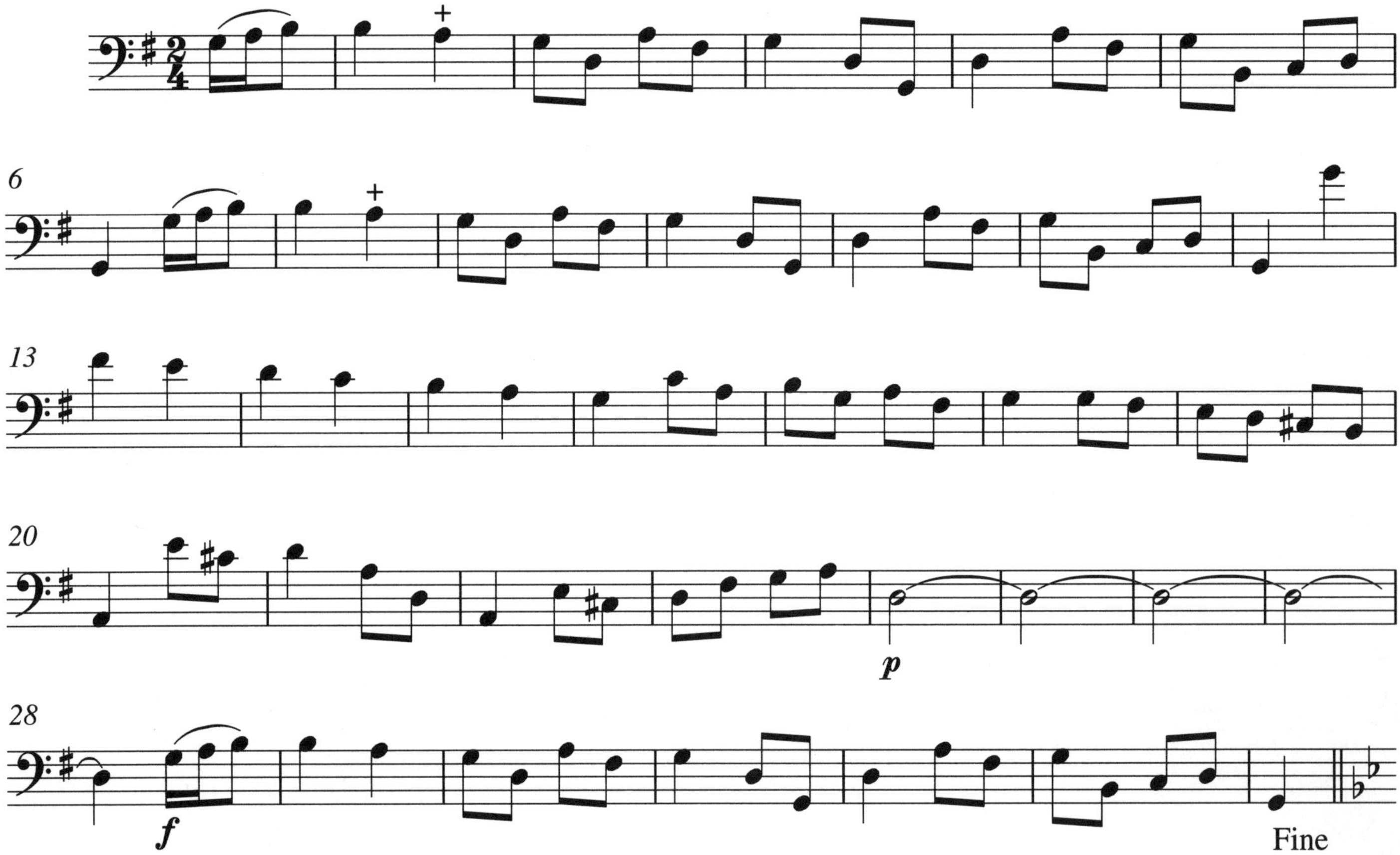

Air 2

© 2006 Schott & Co. Ltd, London

D. C. Air 1 al Fine

14. Contredanses 1 & 2

Contredanse 1

Jean Joseph de Mondonville

Contredanse 2

© 2006 Schott & Co. Ltd, London

D. C. Contredanse 1 al Fine

15. Air

Jean Joseph de Mondonville

Gracieux et gay [♩ = 108]

Notes égales

16. Marche

Jean Joseph de Mondonville

[Grave ♩ = 58]

S&Co.8038 Printed in Germany

1. March pour les matelots

2. Air

3. Rondeau

To be played in rondo form:
sections ABACADA in sequence

Joseph Bodin de Boismortier

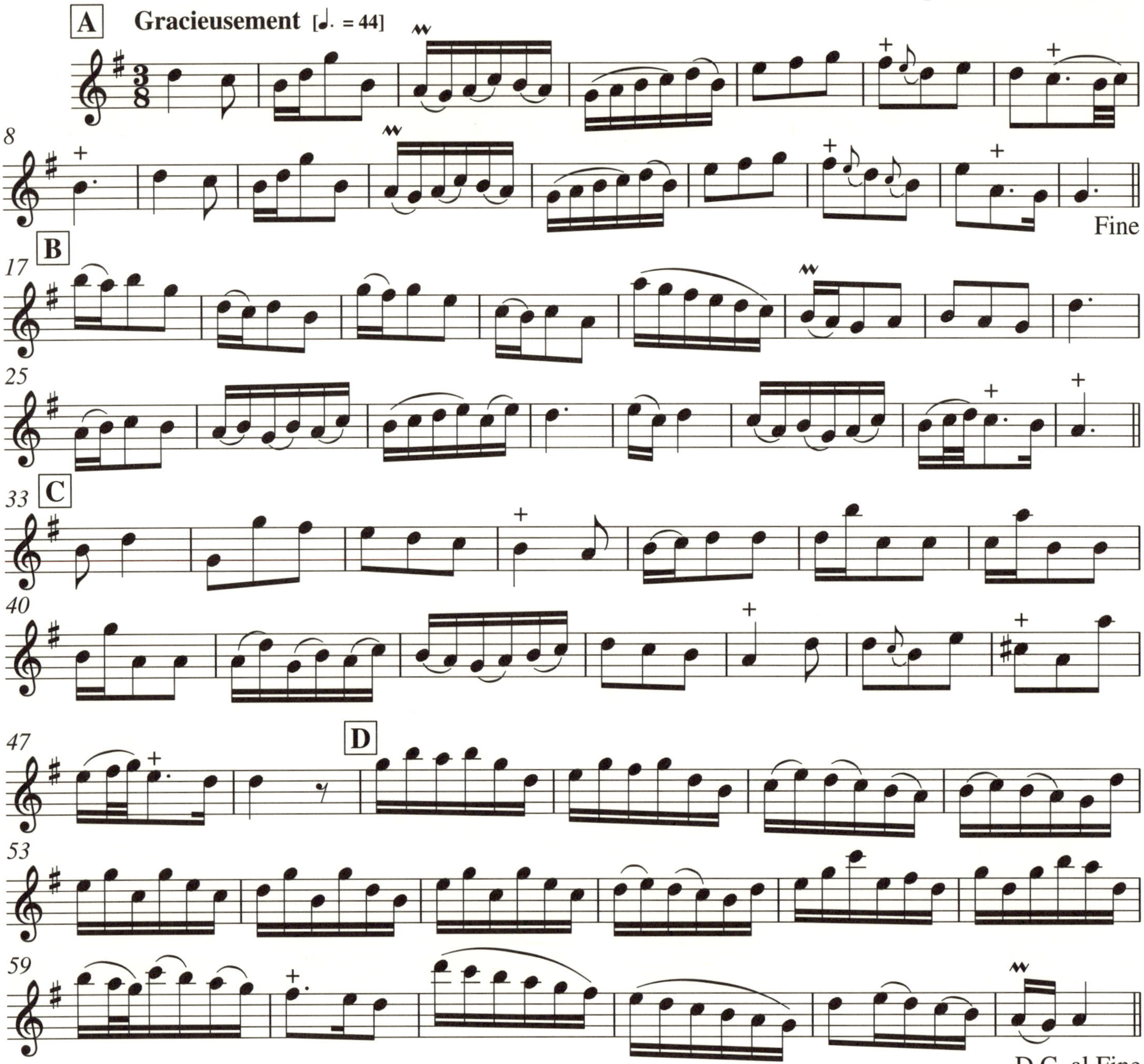

4. Brunette 'Je suis charmé d'une brune'

Michel Pinolet de Montéclair

Double (Variation)

5. Gigues 1 & 2

Michel Corette

Gigue 1

[Lively 2 ♩. = 96]

Gigue 2

Fine

D.C. al Fine

Violin (Flute or Oboe)

6. Vaudeville

Michel Corette

7. Le Menuet à 4–6 coupé

Collected by Charles Nicolas Le Clerc

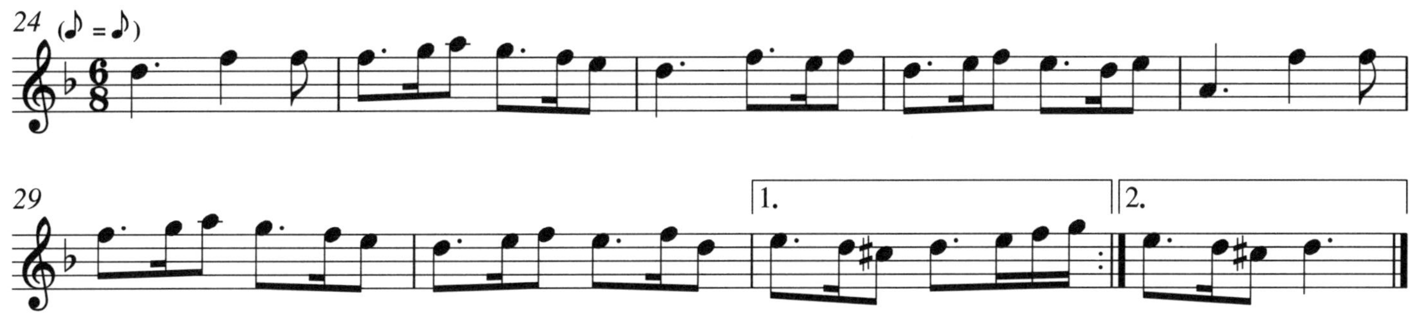

8. La chapelière

Collected by Charles Nicolas Le Clerc

[Steady 2 𝅗𝅥 = 92]

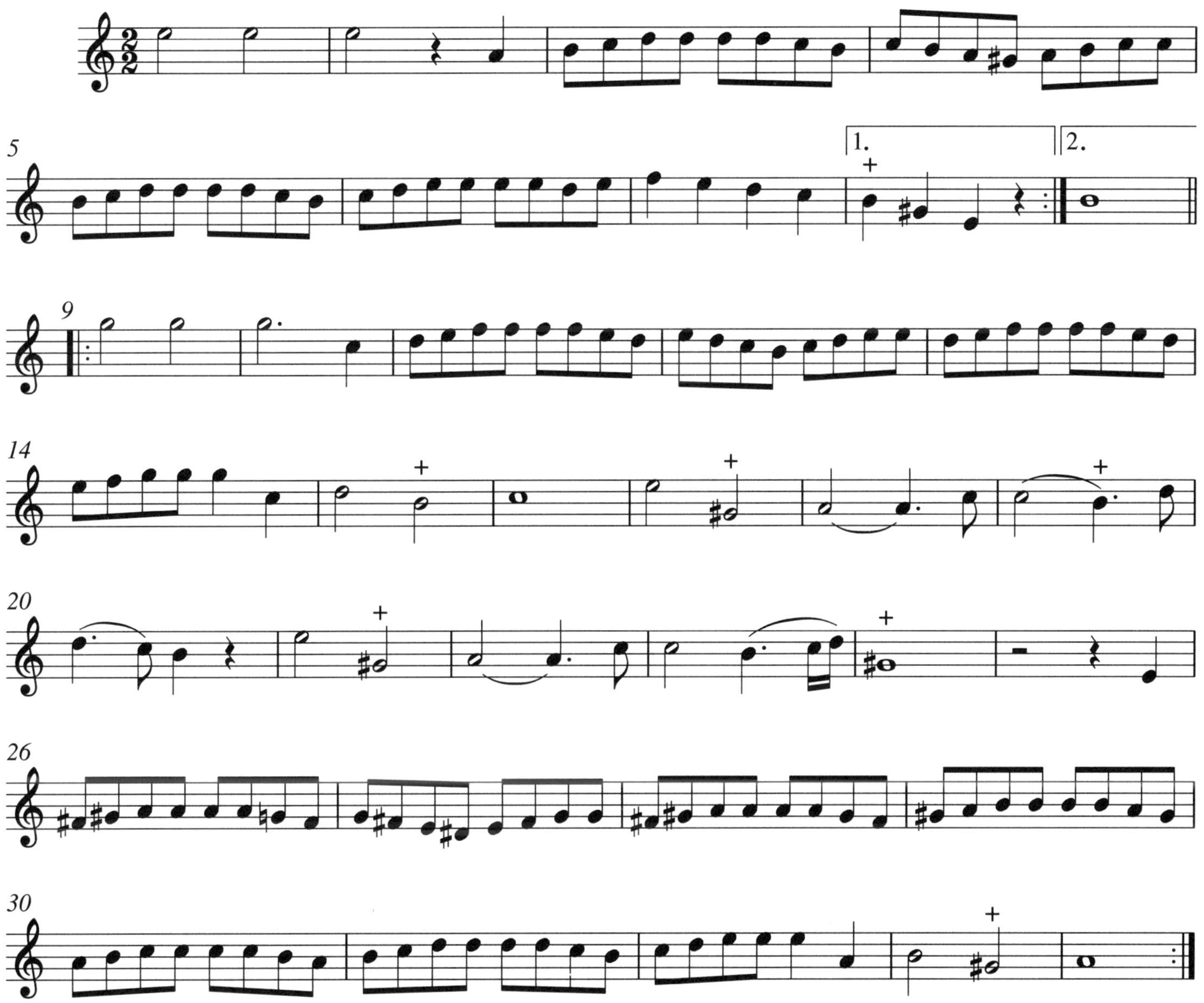

9. Les Grâces et l'enjouement

Collected by Charles Nicolas Le Clerc

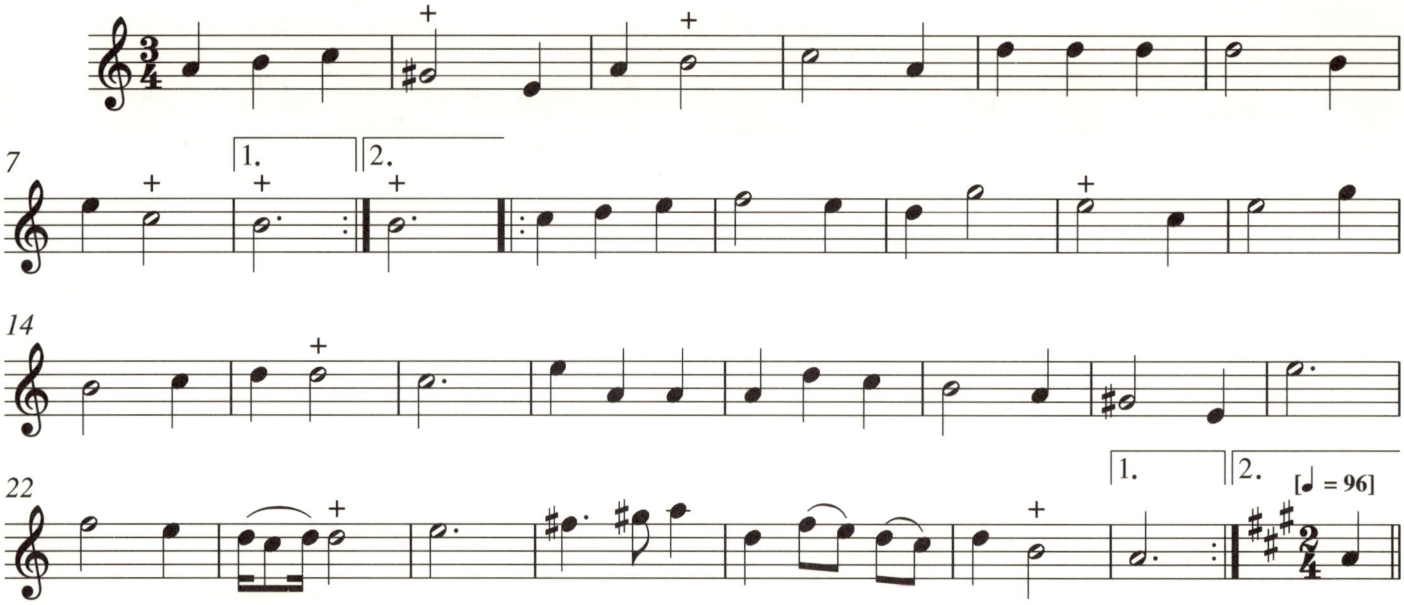

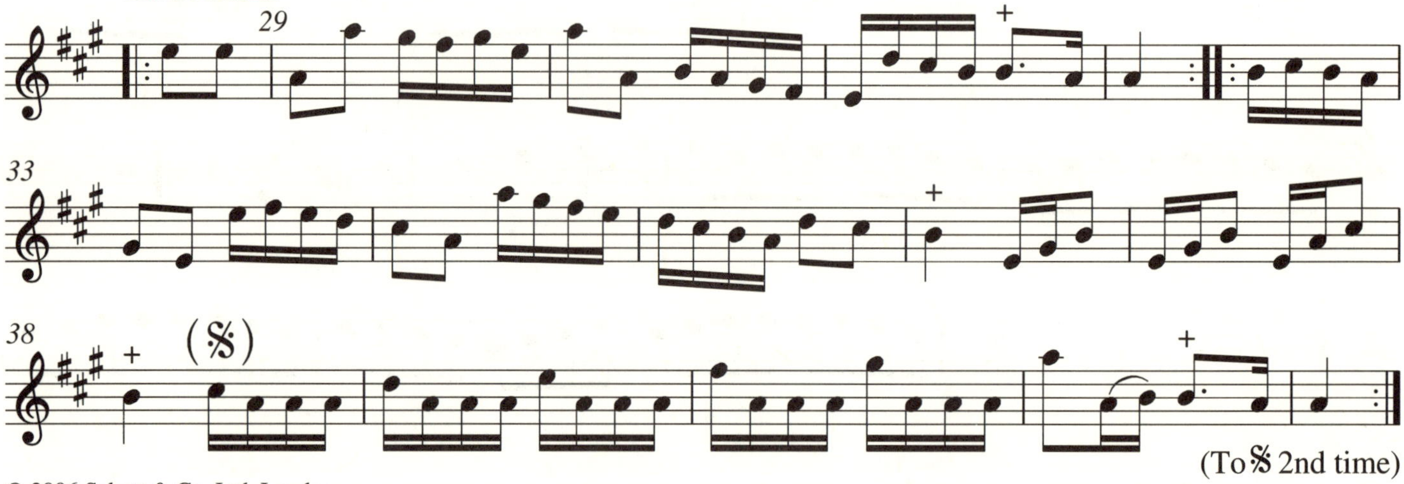

10. La chasse galante

Collected by Charles Nicolas Le Clerc

11. Gavotte and Air

Pierre de Lagarde

12. Branle de Metz

Collected by Leclerc

© 2006 Schott & Co. Ltd, London

13. Airs 1 & 2

Air 1

Jean Joseph de Mondonville

D.C. Air 1 al Fine

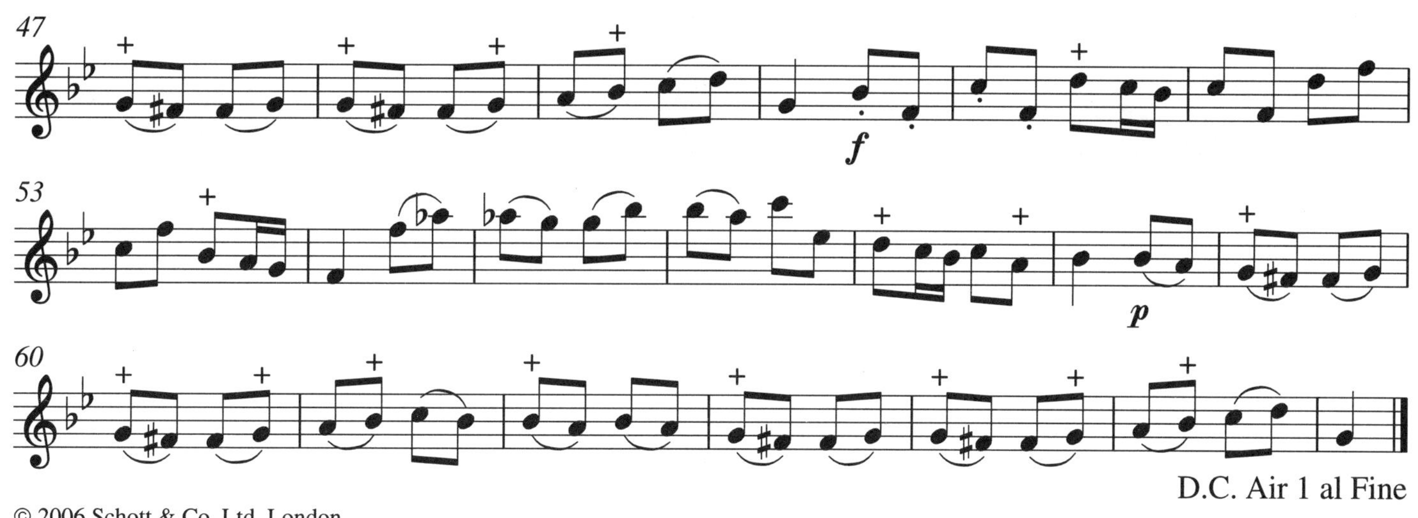

14. Contredanses 1 & 2

Contredanse 1

Jean Joseph de Mondonville

[Lively 2 𝅗𝅥 = 84]

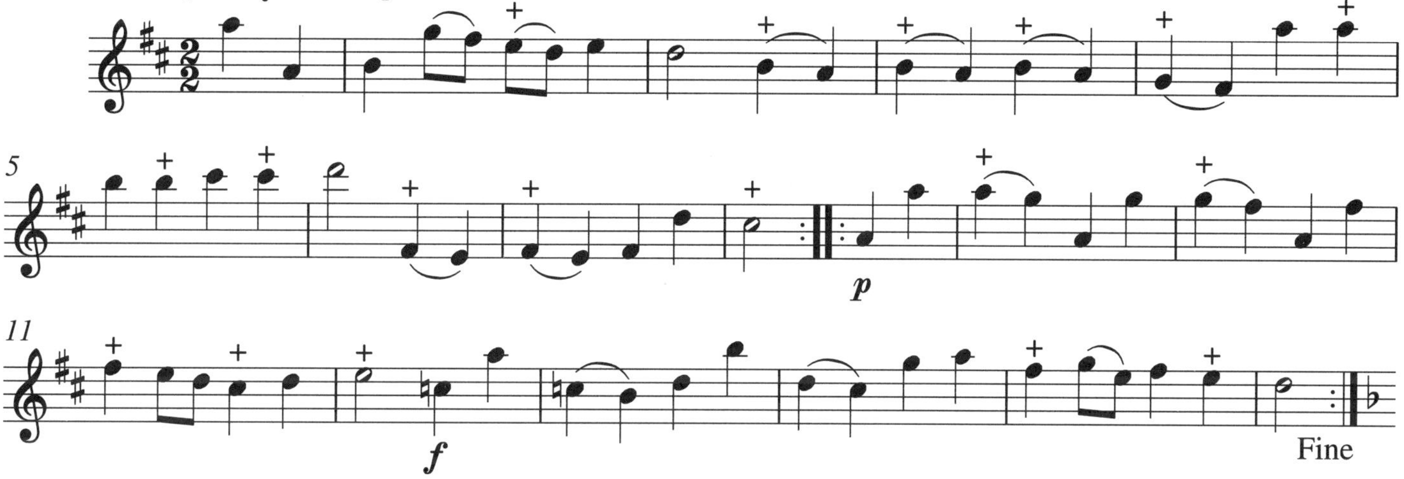

Contredanse 2

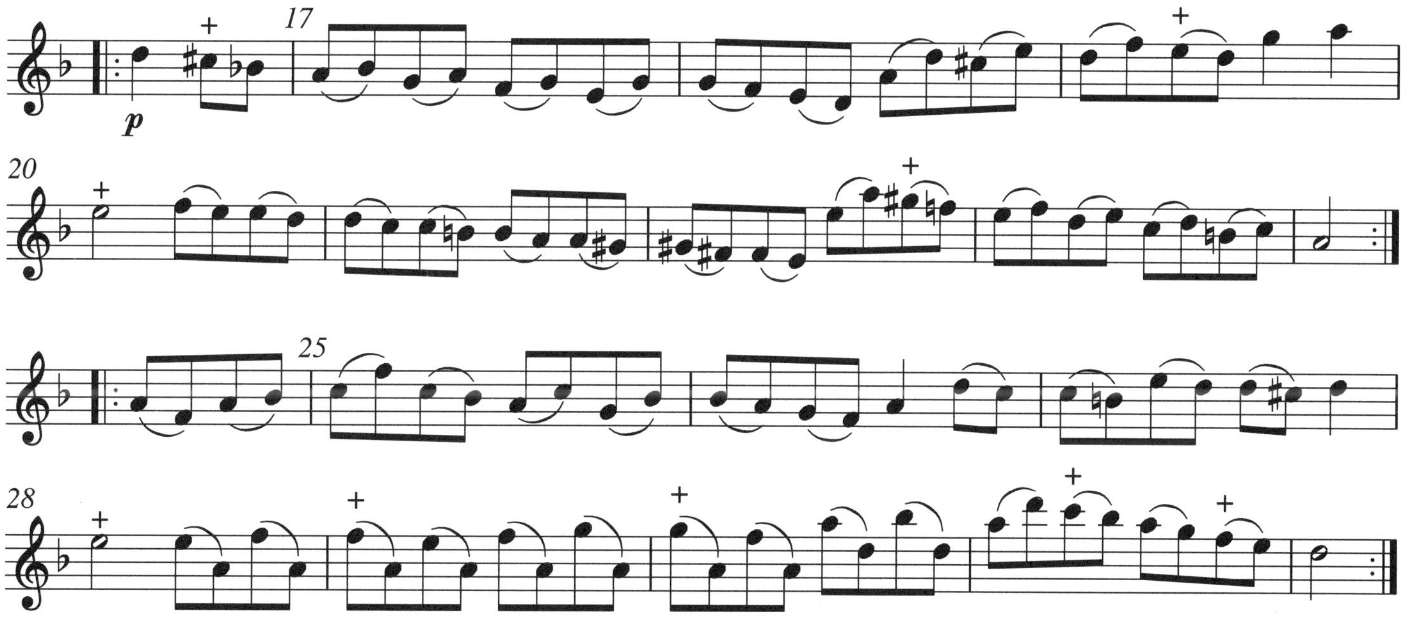

D.C. Contredanse 1 al Fine

15. Air

Jean Joseph de Mondonville

16. Marche

Jean Joseph de Mondonville

[Grave ♩ = 58 **]**

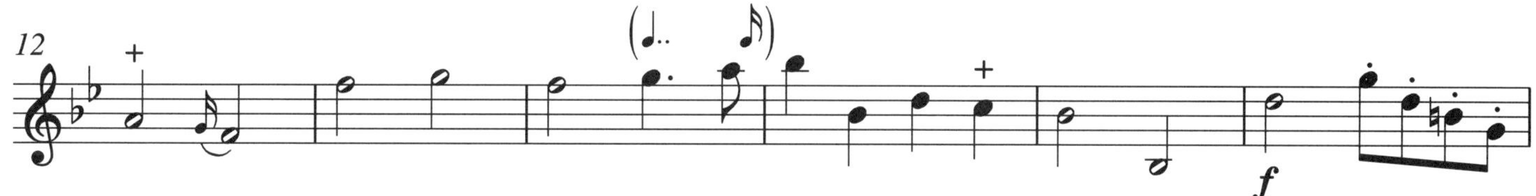

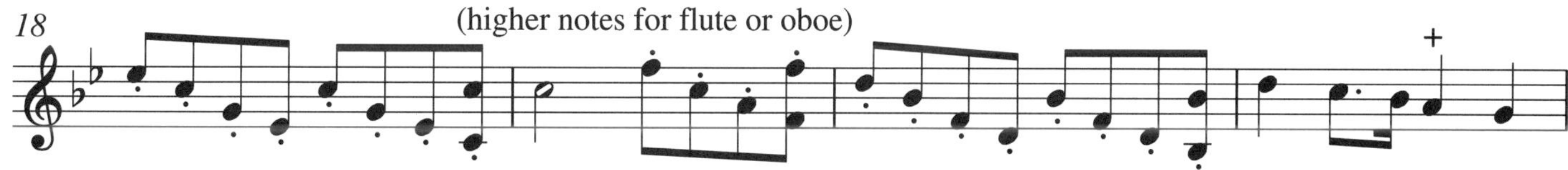

S&Co.8038 Printed in Germany

11. Gavotte and Air

Pierre de Lagarde

Air: Léger

12. Branle de Metz

Collected by Charles Nicolas Le Clerc

13. Airs 1 & 2

Jean Joseph de Mondonville
Air 1
Léger [♩ = 96]
Violin (Flute or Oboe)
Keyboard and optional Cello (Bassoon)
p
p
f
f
Fine

Air 2

14. Contredanses 1 & 2

Jean Joseph de Mondonville

Fine

Contredanse 2

D. C. Contredanse 1 al Fine

15. Air

Jean Joseph de Mondonville

16. Marche

Jean Joseph de Mondonville

S&Co.8038 Printed in Germany

Translation of titles and expressions

Note that similar sounding French and English words may differ subtly or even considerably in meaning.
1. Marche pour les matelots = Sailors' March.
2. Air. Tendre = Tender (loving, delicate).
3. Rondeau = Rondo. Gracieusement = Gracefully.
4. Brunette = Song (see Notes below). Je suis charmé d'une brune = I am captivated by a brunette.
5. Gigues 1 & 2. Gigue = Jig.
6. Vaudeville = Song (see Preface, and Notes below).
7. Le Menuet à 4-6 coupé = Minuet for four to six dancers, in two sections (the meaning of 'coupé' is not entirely clear; the expression might also apply to the dance steps).
8. La chapelière = The hatter.
9. Les Grâces et l'enjouement = The [three] Graces and liveliness (sprightliness, playfulness).
10. La chasse galante = literally, The gallant hunt. But the word 'galant' may mean either 'genteel, courteous', or 'flirtatious, amorous'.
11. Gavotte and Air. Gracieusement sans lenteur = Gracefully without slowness (sluggishness). Léger = Light (nimble, airy).
12. Branle de Metz. Branle (see Notes below) from Metz (a city in eastern France, near to Luxembourg and Germany).
13. Airs 1 & 2. Léger = Light (nimble, airy).
14. Contredanses 1 & 2. 'Contredanse' is a transliteration of 'Country dance'.
15. Air. Gracieux et gai = Graceful and cheerful. For an explanation of 'Notes égales', see below.
16. Marche. Grave = Serious (solemn). Fièrement = Proudly (with spirit or fire).

Übersetzung der Titel und Ausdrücke

1. Marche pour les matelots = Marsch für die Matrosen.
2. Air. Tendre = zärtlich, zart.
3. Rondeau = Rondo. Gracieusement = anmutig.
4. Brunette = ein Lied (s. nachfolgende Anmerkungen). Je suis charmé d'une brune = ich fühle mich zu einem brünetten Mädchen hingezogen.
5. Gigues 1 & 2. Gigue = Jig.
6. Vaudeville = ein Lied (s. Vorwort und nachfolgende Anmerkungen).
7. Le Menuet à 4-6 coupé = ein Menuett für 4 bis 6 Tänzer, in zwei Gruppen (die Bedeutung von ‚coupé' ist nicht völlig eindeutig; der Ausdruck könnte sich genausogut auf die Tanzschritte beziehen).
8. La chapelière = die Hutmacherin.
9. Les Grâces et l'enjouement = die [drei] Grazien und die Lebendigkeit (Elan, Verspieltheit).
10. La chasse galante = wörtlich: die galante Jagd. Aber das Wort ‚galant' kann auch ‚vornehm, höflich' oder ‚kokett, verliebt' heißen.
11. Gavotte and Air. Gracieusement sans lenteur = anmutig, aber ohne Langsamkeit (Trägheit). Léger = leicht (flink, leichtfüßig).
12. Branle de Metz. Branle (s. nachfolgende Anmerkungen) aus Metz (eine Stadt im Osten Frankreichs, in der Nähe von Luxemburg und Deutschland).
13. Airs 1 & 2. Léger = leicht (flink, leichtfüßig).
14. Contredanses 1 & 2. ‚Contredanse' ist eine Transliteration von ‚country dance' (= Volkstanz).
15. Air. Gracieux et gai = Anmutig und fröhlich. Eine Erklärung für ‚Notes égales' folgt im Anschluss.
16. Marche. Grave = ernst (feierlich). Fièrement = stolz (mit Geist oder Feuer).

Notes on the Music and Sources

The music has been edited, with permission, from 18th-century published sources held in the British Library. Bass lines are realised as full keyboard parts; continuo figures are not shown. The signs for trills and other ornaments (see below) and the value and positioning of grace notes are as in the sources. Repeat structures are not always clear in the sources; repeat signs are editorial but dal segno (D.S.) and da capo (D.C.) indications derive from the sources. Well-known dance tunes survive with differing repeat structures, according to the source and choreography. Dynamic indications are original; the sparseness of the latter does not mean that the pieces should be played without dynamic variety. Key signatures have been modernised, apart from in **12** (see below). Editorial tempo indications and metronome marks are suggested in square brackets, but performers should feel free to set their own speeds. Spellings, accents and capitalisation in titles and expression indications have been modernised in the music, but are original in the sources cited below. Other editorial revisions and additions to the music are noted below, after the source for each piece.

Ornamentation plays a vital role in baroque music, especially so in French repertoire. In, for example, Rameau's *Pièces de Clavecin*, one finds many different symbols for different kinds of embellishment, with their uses explained in a table. The pieces in this book rely for the most part on just one sign, '+'. The significance of this sign varies according to context: only a brief mordent, inverted mordent or shake (to start on the upper note if there is time) is possible when it occurs in rapid passages, whereas a more extended trill appears to be needed over some longer notes and at cadences. In **2** and **3** the inverted mordent or shake sign is used as well as '+', though it is hard to see how the two signs are supposed to be differentiated. In **4** the sign 't' is used as well as '+', probably to indicate a trill rather than a mordent or shake. Most grace notes, regardless of their nominal value, may be

La musique et ses sources

Les pièces réunies ici ont été éditées à partir de sources publiées au XVIIIe siècle, avec l'aimable autorisation de la British Library où elles sont conservées. La réalisation des lignes de basse se présente comme une partie de clavier complète, les chiffrages de basse continue n'y apparaissent pas. Les signes indiquant les trilles et les autres ornements (voir ci-dessous) ainsi que la valeur et l'emplacement des notes d'agrément sont fidèles aux sources. Les reprises n'étant pas toujours clairement matérialisées dans les sources, les indications de reprises sont donc ici dues à l'éditeur mais les signes *dal segno* (*D.S.*) et *da capo* (*D.C.*) y sont fidèles. Certains airs de danses très connus présentent des reprises différentes selon les sources et les chorégraphies. Les indications de nuances sont originales, leur rareté ne signifiant aucunement que l'interprétation des pièces soit dépourvue de relief dynamique. Les armures de clefs ont été modernisées, à l'exception de celle du n°**12** (voir ci-dessous). Des indications de tempo ajoutées à l'édition, ainsi que des indications métronomiques, sont suggérées entre crochets, mais l'interprète doit se sentir libre d'établir ses propres tempos. L'orthographe, les accents et les majuscules des titres et les indications d'expression ont été modernisées dans la partition mais sont conformes aux originaux dans les sources citées ci-dessous. Toutes les autres révisions et additions éditoriales effectuées sur la partition sont recensées ci-dessous à la suite de la mention de la source de chaque pièce.

L'ornementation joue un rôle essentiel dans la musique baroque, en particulier dans le répertoire français. Ainsi trouve-t-on dans les *Pièces de clavecin* de Rameau un tableau des nombreux symboles distinctifs correspondant à autant de sortes d'ornements accompagnés d'explications sur leurs usages. Les pièces contenues dans notre recueil ne comportent pour la plupart que le signe « + » dont la signification varie selon le contexte : il peut s'agir d'un pincé bref, d'un pincé renversé (supérieur) ou d'un tremblement (commencé sur la note supérieure si la durée le permet) dans des passages rapides ou d'un trille plus étendu sur des notes plus longues et dans les cadences. Dans les pièces **2** et **3** apparaissent le symbole du pincé renversé et le signe « + », la différenciation entre les deux signes s'avérant toutefois difficile. Dans le n°**4**, le signe « *t* » coexistant avec le signe « + »

Anmerkungen zur Musik und ihren Quellen

Mit Genehmigung der British Library wurden diese Musikstücke, die sich auf im 18. Jahrhundert veröffentlichte Quellen beziehen und in der British Library aufbewahrt werden, herausgegeben. Basslinien sind in vollständig ausgeschriebene Klavierstimmen umgesetzt worden; Generalbassbezifferungen werden nicht angegeben. Die Zeichen für Triller und andere Verzierungen (s. unten) sowie die Länge und Platzierung der Vorschläge sind genauso wie in den Quellen. Die Wiederholungsstrukturen sind in den Quellen nicht immer eindeutig; Wiederholungszeichen sind vom Herausgeber, aber *dal segno* (D.S.)- und *da capo* (D.C.)-Hinweise stammen aus den Quellen. Gut bekannte Tanzmelodien werden meist mit voneinander abweichenden Wiederholungsstrukturen überliefert, je nach Quelle und Choreographie. Die dynamischen Hinweise sind original aber deren spärliches Vorkommen bedeutet nicht, dass die Stücke ohne dynamische Abwechslung gespielt werden sollen. Die Tonarten sind, außer in Nr. **12** (s. unten) modernisiert worden. Tempohinweise vom Herausgeber und Metronomangaben werden in eckigen Klammern vorgeschlagen, aber Vortragende sollten sich frei fühlen, ihre eigene Geschwindigkeit zu wählen. Rechtschreibung, Betonung und Groß- und Kleinschreibung bei Titeln und Ausdruckshinweisen sind modernisiert worden, aber in den Quellen, die unten zitiert werden, sind sie original. Weitere Hinweise auf Überarbeitungen und Zusätze durch den Herausgeber stehen ebenfalls unten, nach der Quellangabe für jedes Musikstück.

Die Verzierungskunst spielt eine überaus wichtige Rolle in der Barockmusik, besonders im französischen Repertoire. In Rameaus *Pièces de Clavecin*, zum Beispiel, findet man viele unterschiedliche Symbole für verschiedene Ausschmückungen, deren Gebrauch in einer Tabelle erklärt wird. Die Stücke in diesem Band beziehen sich zum größten Teil auf nur ein Zeichen, das ‚+'. Die Bedeutung dieses Zeichens verändert sich je nach dem Zusammenhang: sowohl ein kurzer Mordent [= Wechsel mit der unteren Nebennote, Anm.d.Ü.], ein Pralltriller oder ein kurzer Triller (von der oberen Note aus zu beginnen, wenn zeitlich machbar) ist möglich, wenn es in schnellen Passagen auftaucht. Über längeren Noten und in Kadenzen hingegen wird augenscheinlich ein längerer Triller notwendig. In Nr. **2** und **3** wird außer dem ‚+' auch das Pralltriller- und das Trillerzeichen ver-

interpreted either as appoggiaturas played on the beat and taking half the value or less of the note that follows, or (especially when filling an interval of a third) as short notes played on or just before the beat. Occasionally the positioning of a grace note in the score may suggest its rhythmic placement (see **4**). Interpretations of ornaments on the CD may provide a useful guide, but they are not intended to be prescriptive.

indique probablement l'exécution d'un trille de préférence à un pincé ou à un tremblement. La plupart des agréments, quelle que soit leur durée, peuvent être exécutés comme des appogiatures jouées sur le temps et remplissant la moitié, ou moins, de la valeur de la note qui suit ou (surtout placés entre les deux degrés d'une tierce) comme des notes brèves jouées sur le temps ou juste avant. Il arrive que la position d'un agrément dans la partition renseigne sur sa réalisation rythmique (voir n°**4**). L'interprétation des ornements sur le CD fournira un guide utile mais ne se veut aucunement directive.

wendet, obwohl die Unterschiede zwischen den beiden Zeichen nicht ganz einfach zu erkennen sind. In der Nr. **4** wird sowohl das Zeichen ‚t' als auch ‚+' verwendet, wahrscheinlich um eher einen Triller als ein Mordent oder einen Kurztriller anzuzeigen. Die meisten kleingedruckten Noten können, unabhängig von ihrem Nominalwert, entweder als Vorschläge interpretiert und auf den Schlag gespielt werden, wobei sie von der Länge her die Hälfte oder weniger des Wertes der nachfolgenden Note ausmachen. Oder sie werden als kurze Noten (vor allem, wenn sie eine Terz ergeben) auf oder kurz vor dem Schlag gespielt. Gelegentlich weisen die Positionen von kleingedruckten Noten in der Partitur auch auf ihre rhythmische Eingliederung hin (s. Nr. **4**). Die Ausführungen von Verzierungen auf der CD können ein nützlicher Führer sein, aber sie sind nicht verbindlich.

Another characteristic of the French style is the use of *notes inégales*. In pairs of quavers, for example, the first of each pair may be played a little longer and stronger than the second, giving a slightly 'swung' effect (to use a jazz expression). The unevenness must not be mechanical or tedious. In **15** the countermanding instruction 'notes égales' is given, though it is not clear if this applies just to the opening pair of quavers with the staccato dots, to equivalent upbeats elsewhere, or to quavers without slurs generally.

Le style français se caractérise aussi par la pratique des « notes inégales ». Ainsi, de deux croches, la durée de la première sera légèrement plus longue et son attaque plus forte que celles de la deuxième, donnant un effet légèrement balancé (comme le *swing*, pour utiliser un terme de jazz). Cette inégalité ne doit pas être mécanique ni fastidieuse. Dans le n°**15** figure la contre-consigne « *notes égales* » sans que soit clairement indiqué si celle-ci s'applique aux deux croches initiales comportant des points de *staccato*, aux anacrouses équivalentes du reste du morceau ou aux croches dépourvues de liaison en général.

Eine andere Eigenart des französischen Stils ist der Gebrauch von *notes inégales*. Bei paarweise vorkommenden Achtelnoten zum Beispiel, wird die erste jeden Paares ein kleines bisschen länger und stärker gespielt als die zweite, wodurch ein leicht ‚geschwungener' Effekt erreicht wird (um einen Jazzausdruck zu benutzen). Diese Ungleichheit darf aber nicht mechanisch oder langweilig klingen. In Nr. **15** wird die entgegengesetzte Anweisung, *notes égales*, gegeben, aber es wird nicht klar, ob sie sich nur auf die eröffnenden Achtelpaare mit den Staccatopunkten beziehen, auf entsprechende Auftakte an anderen Stellen, oder auf Achtelnoten ohne Bindungen ganz allgemein.

1. This tune was used for several stage and ballroom choreographies in the early 18th century. In the 20th century the tune became known in Britain as a Christmas Carol, 'Masters in this hall', arranged by Gustav Holst. The version here, a march for sailors, comes from Act III of the opera *Alcione* by Marin Marais (1656–1728), a composer best known for his many viola da gamba compositions.

1. Cet air servit dans plusieurs chorégraphies de scène et de salon au début du XVIIIe siècle. Au XXe siècle, sa version de chant de Noël, *Masters in this hall*, et son arrangement par Gustav Holst le rendirent célèbre en Grande-Bretagne. La version retenue ici, une marche de marins, provient de l'acte III de l'opéra *Alcione* de Marin Marais (1656–1728), compositeur plus connu pour ses nombreuses compositions pour la viole de gambe.

1. Diese Melodie wurde für mehrere Bühnen- und Ballchoreographien im frühen 18. Jahrhundert benutzt. Im 20. Jahrhundert wurde die Melodie in Britannien als Weihnachtslied unter dem Namen ‚Masters in this hall' bekannt. Das Arrangement war von Gustav Holst. Die hier vorliegende Fassung, ein Marsch für Matrosen, stammt aus dem III. Akt der Oper *Alcione* von Marin Marais (1656–1728), einem Komponisten, der vor allem für seine vielen Kompositionen für die Viola da Gamba bekannt ist.

Source: *Alcione, Tragédie* by Marais (Paris, 1706). BL K.5.b.23. The score also indicates a 'tambourin' (translatable as either tambourine or two-headed tambour) to be played on the first beat of every bar.

Source : *Alcione*, tragédie par Marin Marais (Paris, 1706). BL K.5b.23. La partition indique également qu'un « tambourin » (qui pouvait aussi être un tambour à double peau) devait marquer le premier temps de chaque mesure.

Quelle: *Alcione, Tragédie* von Marais (Paris, 1706). BL K.5.b.23 [BL = British Library, Anm. d. Ü.]. Die Partitur verzeichnet auch ein 'tambourin' (entweder als Tamburin oder beidseitig bespannte Trommel übersetzbar), das auf dem ersten Schlag eines jeden Taktes zu spielen ist.

2, 3. The prolific composer Joseph Bodin de Boismortier (1689–1755) produced over 50 collections of instrumental pieces. Many of them, like

2, 3. Joseph Bodin de Boismortier (1689–1755), compositeur prolifique, produisit plus de cinquante recueils de pièces instrumentales. Nombre

2, 3. Der profilierte Komponist Joseph Bodin de Boismortier (1689–1755) produzierte über 50 Sammlungen mit Instrumentalstücken. Viele von

the pieces here, are designed to be played on a wide variety of instruments, including drawing-room versions of the bagpipe and hurdy-gurdy (musette and vieille) popular in 18th-century France.

Source: *Il Divertissemens de Campagne pour une Musette ou Viele seule Avec la Basse Qui conviennent aux Flûtes à bec, Flûtes traversieres, Violons, ou Hautbois* by Boismortier, Op. 49 (Paris, 1734). BL g.96.(3.). Slurs are mainly editorial; exceptions include links between grace notes and principal notes, and those in bars 7, 17–20, 22, 31, 47, 64 of the Rondeau.

4. In 18th-century France the word 'brunette' described a light song of unrequited love, similar in character to some vaudevilles and often, as in this case, about a woman with brown hair. The lyric goes:

Je suis charmé d'une Brune
qui tient mon ame en langueur:
Quelle seroit ma fortune!
Si j'avois touché son coeur.
Ah! que ma flame est
    importune!
Jamais Amour n'est sans
    douleur.

The collection from which this song is taken was intended to be sung or played. Michel Pinolet de Montéclair (1667–1737) worked in Italy before settling in Paris in 1702, where he played the double bass at the Opéra. His works include opera, opera-ballets and chamber cantatas.

Source: *Brunetes Anciènes et Modernes. Aproprié à la Flute Traversière avec une Basse d'Accompagnement* by Montéclair, first collection (Paris, c.1720). BL C.23. Slurs for the quavers in the variation, apart from in bars 25, 29, 39 and over the minim in bar 47, are editorial.

5, 6. Michel Corrette (1709–1795) earned his living primarily as an organist. As well as composing for the theatre, Corrette produced many sacred works, including a setting of Psalm 148 (Laudate Dominum) based on the music of 'Spring' from Vivaldi's *Four Seasons*. The pieces here come from a collection of songs and dances performed at the Thêatre de la Foire Saint Laurent during 1733.

---

d'entre elles, comme celles-ci, peuvent être jouées sur une grande diversité d'instruments dont des modèles de salon de la cornemuse, de la musette et de la vielle en faveur en France au XVIIIe siècle.

Source : *Il Divertissemens de Campagne pour une musette ou Viele seule Avec la Basse Qui conviennent aux Flûtes à bec, Flûtes traversieres, Violons, ou Hautbois* de Boismortier, Op.49 (Paris, 1734). BL g.96.(3.). Les liaisons de phrasé sont principalement dues à l'éditeur, à l'exception de celles liant les agréments et les notes principales et de celles des mesures 7, 17–20, 22,31, 47, 64.

4. En France, au XVIIIe siècle, le terme de « brunette » désignait une chanson d'amour malheureux, au caractère léger semblable à celui de certains vaudevilles, et évoquant souvent, comme c'est le cas ici, une femme aux cheveux bruns :

Je suis charmé d'une Brune
Qui tient mon âme en langueur
Quelle seroit ma fortune !
Si j'avois touché son cœur.
Ah ! Que ma flame est
    importune !
Jamais Amour n'est sans
    douleur.

Le recueil dont est extraite cette chanson était destiné au chant ou au jeu instrumental. Michel Pinolet de Montéclair (1667–1737) travailla en Italie avant de s'installer à Paris en 1702 où il jouait de la contrebasse à l'Opéra. Ses œuvres comprennent des opéras, des opéras-ballets et des cantates de chambre.

Source : *Brunetes Anciènes et Modernes. Aproprié à la Flute Traversière avec une Basse d'Accompagnement* de Montéclair, premier recueil (Paris vers 1720). BL C.23. Les liaisons de phrasé des croches dans la variation sont dues à l'éditeur, sauf dans les mesures 25, 29, 39 et sur la blanche de la mesure 47.

5, 6. Michel Corrette (1709–1795) gagna principalement sa vie comme organiste. A côté de sa musique de théâtre, Corrette produisit de nombreuses œuvres sacrées dont une mise en musique du Psaume 148 (*Laudate Dominum*) sur le concerto «Le Printemps» extrait des *Quatre saisons* de Vivaldi. Ces pièces proviennent d'un recueil de chansons et de danses exécutées au Thêâtre de la Foire

---

ihnen, wie diese Stücke hier, sind so angelegt, dass sie von vielen verschiedenen Instrumenten gespielt werden können. Dazu gehören auch Salonfassungen von Dudelsack und Drehorgel (Musette und Vieille), die im Frankreich des 18. Jahrhunderts beliebt waren.

Quelle: *Il Divertissements de Campagne pour une Musette ou Viele seule Avec la Basse Qui conviennent aux Flûtes à bec, Flûtes traversieres, Violons, ou Hautbois* von Boismortier, Op. 49 (Paris, 1734). BL g.96.(3.). Bindungen sind hauptsächlich vom Herausgeber ; Ausnahmen sind die Bindungen zwischen den Vorschlägen und Hauptnoten, und jene in den Takten 7, 17–20, 22, 31, 47 und 64 des Rondeaus.

4. Im Frankreich des 18. Jahrhunderts beschrieb das Wort ‚brunette' ein leichtes Lied über unerwiderte Liebe. Diese waren in der Art einiger Vaudevilles sehr ähnlich und darüber hinaus, wie in diesem Fall, über eine Frau mit braunen Haaren. Der Text ist wie folgt:

Je suis charmé d'une Brune
qui tient mon ame en langueur:
Quelle seroit ma fortune!
Si j'avois touché son coeur.
Ah! que ma flame est
    importune!
Jamais Amour n'est sans
    douleur.

Die Sammlung, aus der dieses Lied entnommen wurde, war darauf ausgerichtet, gesungen oder gespielt zu werden. Michel Pinolet de Montéclair (1667–1737) arbeitete in Italien, bevor er sich 1702 in Paris niederließ. Dort spielte er Kontrabass an der Oper. Sein Werk umfassen Opern, Opernballette und Kammerkantaten.

Quelle: *Brunetes Anciènes et Modernes. Aproprié à la Flute Traversière avec une Basse d'Accompagnement* von Montéclair, erste Sammlung (Paris, ca. 1720). BL C.23. Die Bindungen für die Achtelnoten in der Variation sind vom Herausgeber, außer in den Takten 25, 29, 39 und über der halben Note in Takt 47.

5, 6. Michel Corrette (1709–1795) verdiente seinen Lebensunterhalt in erster Linie als Organist. Daneben komponierte er nicht nur für das Theater, sondern verfasste auch viele geistliche Werke, einschließlich einer Vertonung des Psalms 148 (Laudate Dominum), deren Grundlage der ‚Frühling' aus den *Vier Jahreszeiten* von Vivaldi ist. Die Stücke in diesem Buch stammen aus einer

The vaudeville ends the score, and the lyrics describe the need for novelty in musical composition:

Lors que l'on met dans un
    ouvrage
Quelque lueur de Nouveauté
C'est un glorieux avantage
Mais c'est la difficulté
Dans ce temps cy l'on ne fait
    autre chose
Que de donner au vieux un
    autre habit
En vers et prose
Tout est dit.

Source: *Recueil de Divertissements de l'Opera Comique*, Op. 9, by Corrette (Paris, 1733). BL B.386. bb.(2.) In the original score, the three-part writing of the second gigue is scored for two flutes on the upper parts and violins on the lower part. Slurs in the Vaudeville are editorial.

7, 8, 9, 10, 12. Charles Nicolas Le Clerc (1697–1774) was a leading music publisher in Paris; he published many collections of contredanses. The music is often taken, unattributed, from ballets and instrumental works by well-known composers of the day. Older tunes occur too; the 'Branle de Metz' (**12**) has a modal flavour, and is similar in character to branles of the 16th century (the branle was a line or circle dance, with steps to the left and then to the right in its basic form).

Source: *Troisième Recueil de Contredanses ... Recueilly et mis en Ordre par Mr. Le Clerc* (Paris, 1737). BL h.422.a.(1.). Slurs are editorial, except in **8**. The original key signature of one flat has been retained in **12**, because the piece is in the dorian and not the minor mode. The petite reprise is **9** is editorial.

11. Music by Pierre de Lagarde (1717–1791) for four stage works has survived; they include the one-act ballet *Aeglé* from which these two pieces are taken. According to the title page, the ballet was performed before the king at Versailles in 1748 and 1750, and again at the Théâtre de l'Académie Royale de Musique in 1751. The Air follows the Gavotte

---

Saint Laurent au cours de l'année 1733. Les paroles du vaudeville qui conclut la partition soulignent la nécessité de la nouveauté dans la composition musicale :

Lors que l'on met dans un
    ouvrage
Quelque lueur de Nouveauté
C'est un glorieux avantage
Mais c'est la difficulté
Dans ce temps cy l'on ne fait
    autre chose
Que de donner au vieux un
    autre habit
En vers et prose
Tout est dit.

Source : *Recueil de Divertissements de l'Opera Comique*, Op.9, de Corrette (Paris, 1733). BL B.386. bb.(2.).Dans la partition originale, l'écriture à trois voix de la deuxième gigue est instrumentée pour deux flûtes aux parties supérieures et pour des violons à la partie inférieure. Les liaisons de phrasé du vaudeville sont de l'éditeur.

7, 8, 9, 10, 12. Charles Nicolas Le Clerc (1697–1774) était un grand éditeur de musique de Paris. Il publia de nombreux recueils de contredanses dont la musique était souvent extraite, sans être attribuée, de ballets et d'œuvres instrumentales de compositeurs célèbres de l'époque. Des airs plus anciens y apparaissent également, comme le *Branle de Metz* aux inflexions modales et de caractère semblable aux branles du XVIe siècle (dans sa forme la plus simple, le branle était dansé en ligne ou en cercle avec des pas vers la gauche, puis vers la droite).

Source : *Troisième Recueil de Contredanses…Recueilly et mis en ordre par Mr Le Clerc*, (Paris, 1737). BL h.422.a.(1.). Les liaisons de phrasé sont de l'éditeur sauf celles du n°**8**. L'armure originale d'un bémol à la clef a été maintenue dans le n° **12** car la pièce est en mode dorien et non en mineur. La *petite reprise* indiquée dans le n°**9** a été ajoutée à l'édition.

11. Quatre œuvres scéniques de Pierre de Lagarde (1717–1791) ont survécu parmi lesquelles le ballet en un acte *Aeglé* dont sont extraites ces deux pièces. La page de titre précise que ce ballet fut représenté devant le roi à Versailles en 1748 et en 1750, puis de nouveau au Théâtre de l'Académie Royale de Musique en 1751. L'*Air* fait suite à la *Gavotte* sur un

---

Sammlung mit Liedern und Tänzen, die im Jahr 1733 am Théâtre de la Foire Saint Laurent aufgeführt wurden. Die Musik endet mit einem Vaudeville, dessen Text die Notwendigkeit nach Neuerungen in musikalischen Kompositionen beschreibt:

Lors que l'on met dans un
    ouvrage
Quelque lueur de Nouveauté
C'est un glorieux avantage
Mais c'est la difficulté
Dans ce temps cy l'on ne fait
    autre chose
Que de donner au vieux un
    autre habit
En vers et prose
Tout est dit.

Quelle: *Recueil de Divertissements de l'Opera Comique*, Op. 9, von Corrette (Paris, 1733). BL B.383. bb (2.). In der Originalpartitur ist die dreistimmige zweite Gigue in den oberen Stimmen für zwei Flöten und in den unteren Stimme für eine Geige gesetzt. Die Bindungen im Vaudeville sind vom Herausgeber.

7, 8, 9, 10, 12. Charles Nicolas Le Clerc (1697–1774) war ein führender Musikherausgeber in Paris; er veröffentlichte viele Sammlungen mit Contretänzen. Die Musik wurde oft unverändert aus Balletten und Instrumentalwerken von zur damaligen Zeit bekannten Komponisten übernommen. Ältere Melodien kommen auch vor; der ‚Branle de Metz' (Nr. **12**) hat einen modalen Anstrich und ist von der Art her den Bransles des 16. Jahrhunderts sehr ähnlich (der Bransle war ein Reihen- oder Kreistanz, mit Grundschritten nach links und dann nach rechts).

Quelle: *Troisième Recueil de Contredanses … Recueilly et mis in Ordre par Mr. Le Clerc* (Paris, 1737). BL h.422.a.(1.). Die Bindungen sind vom Herausgeber, außer in Nr. **8**. Das Originalvorzeichen, ein b, wurde in Nr. **12** beibehalten, weil das Stück nicht in Moll steht, sondern dorisch ist. Die kleine Reprise in Nr. **9** ist vom Herausgeber.

11. Die Musik von Pierre de Lagarde (1717–1791) für vier Bühnenwerke ist erhalten geblieben; sie schließt das einaktige Ballett *Aeglé* mit ein, aus dem diese beiden Musikstücke entnommen sind. Der Titelseite zufolge wurde das Ballett 1748 und 1750 in Versailles vor dem König aufgeführt, und dann noch einmal 1751 im Théâtre de l'Academie

on the same page of the score; the two pieces may be played in sequence or separately.

Source: *ÆGLÉ, Ballet en un acte* by Lagarde (Paris, c.1751). BL G.653.a.(2.). Slurs and articulation marks are original, with some editorial additions for consistency. The vertical dashes are a sign for staccato. The tied notes in the keyboard right hand, bars 1–2 and 4–6, are from the original score, as are the lower notes of the right hand in bars 29–33. The repeat indications in the second half of the Gavotte are editorial.

13, 14, 15, 16. Jean Joseph de Mondonville (1711–1772) came from a noble but poor family. During the 1730s he developed a reputation in Paris as a violinist and composer, and he then went on to write music for a number of stage works in the 1740s and 50s. The pieces here are from the 'ballet heroïque', *Le Carnaval de Parnasse* (1749).

Source: *Le Carnaval de Parnasse, Ballet Heroïque*, Op. 7, by Mondonville (Paris, c. 1749). BL G.653.a.(1.). In these pieces, slurs and articulation marks have been left exactly as in the original score. There are occasional minor inconsistencies that players may want to reconcile (see the introductory remarks). The March **16** marks the entrance of Euterpe, Momus and L'Amour. The keyboard right hand in **14** bars 2–12 (first note) is indicated as orchestral filling in the original score.

seul feuillet de la partition originale. Ces deux pièces peuvent être jouées l'une après l'autre ou isolément.

Source : *ÆGLÉ, Ballet en un acte de Lagarde (Paris, vers 1751).* BL G.653.a.(2.). Les liaison et indications de phrasé sont originales et comportent quelques ajouts éditoriaux par souci de cohérence. Les tirets verticaux indiquent le *staccato*. Les notes liées de la main droite de clavier des mesures 1–2 et 4–6 figurent sur la partition originale ainsi que les notes inférieures de la main droite des mesures 29 à 33. Les indications de reprise dans la deuxième moitié de la *Gavotte* ont été ajoutées à l'édition.

13, 14, 15, 16. Jean Joseph de Mondonville (1711–1722) était issu d'une famille noble mais pauvre. Au cours de la décennie de 1730, il acquit une certaine réputation à Paris en tant que violoniste et compositeur et écrivit ensuite, au cours des années 1740 et 1750, la musique de nombreuses œuvres scéniques. Ces pièces appartiennent au « ballet héroïque » extrait du *Carnaval de Parnasse* (1749).

Source : *Le Carnaval de Parnasse, Ballet Héroïque*, Op.7 de Mondonville (Paris, vers 1749). BL G.653.a.(1.). Les liaisons et phrasés de ces pièces sont exactement conformes à la partition originale. Quelques incohérences mineures seront facilement rectifiées par les interprètes (voir les commentaires d'introduction). La *Marche* n°**16** marque l'entrée d'Euterpe, de Momus et de l'Amour. Dans la pièce n°**14**, la main droite de la partie de clavier des mesures 2 à 12 (première note) est notée comme un remplissage orchestral dans la partition originale.

Royale de Musique. Die Air folgt direkt auf die Gavotte auf derselben Partiturseite; die beiden Stücke können zusammen oder getrennt gespielt werden.
Quelle: *AÉGLE, Ballet en un acte von Lagarde* (Paris, ca. 1751). BL G.653. a.(2.). Bindungen und Artikulationszeichen sind original, mit einigen herausgeberischen Zusätzen, um die Folgerichtigkeit aufrecht zu erhalten. Die senkrechten Striche sind Staccatozeichen. Die gebundenen Noten in der rechten Hand des Klavierparts, Takte 1–2 und 4–6, sind aus der Originalpartitur, genauso wie die tiefen Töne der rechten Hand in den Takten 29–33. Die Wiederholungszeichen in der zweiten Hälfte der Gavotte sind vom Herausgeber.

13, 14, 15, 16. Jean Joseph de Mondonville (1711–1772) stammte aus einer adeligen aber armen Familie. Während der 30er- Jahre des 18. Jahrhunderts erarbeitete er sich in Paris einen Ruf als Geiger und Komponist, und schrieb dann in den darauffolgenden 40er- und 50er- Jahren die Musik für eine ganze Anzahl von Bühnenwerken. Die Musikstücke hier sind alle aus dem ‚ballet heroïque', *Le Carnaval de Parnasse* (1749).
Quelle: *Le Carnaval de Parnasse, Ballet Heroïque*, Op. 7, von Mondonville (Paris, ca. 1749). BL G.653. a.(1.). In diesen Stücken wurden die Bindungen und Artikulationszeichen genauso belassen wie in der Originalpartitur. Gelegentlich gibt es kleinere Unstimmigkeiten, die die Spieler selbst ausgleichen mögen (s. die einleitenden Bemerkungen). Der Marsch Nr. **16** markiert das Erscheinen von Euterpe, Momus und Amor. In der Nr. **14** ist die rechte Hand der Klavierstimme in den Takten 2–12 (erste Note) in der Originalpartitur als Orchesterfüllmaterial angegeben.

About the performers

The CD that accompanies this book was recorded by THE BROADSIDE BAND in January 2006, at Trinity College of Music, The Old Royal Naval College, Greenwich, London.

Recording engineer: Morgan Roberts
Executive producer: Simon Weir
Music director: Jeremy Barlow

The recording incorporates a Roland C-80 digital harpsichord, provided by Chamberlain Music (www.chamberlain-music.com). The instrument was recorded acoustically with the other performers, and simultaneously on a separate channel for the play-along tracks.

Instrumentalists:

SHARON LINDO *violin*
Sharon performs, records and tours with many established medieval, renaissance, baroque and folk groups, including The Broadside Band, The Sixteen, The Dufay Collective, Collegium Musicum 90, Sirinu and The New Scorpion Band. She leads the Corelli Orchestra in Cheltenham and has toured with Shakespeare's Globe in Japan, Italy and America.

JENNIFER STINTON *flute*
As a student Jenny won several scholarships and awards at the Royal Academy of Music. She then signed a contract with Collins Classics and recorded twelve CDs for the label, covering the major works of the flute repertoire. In 1991 she performed a Mozart flute concerto at the Royal Festival Hall, London, with the Philharmonia Orchestra, in the presence of Diana, Princess of Wales.

NICK STRINGFELLOW *cello*
Nick studied at Chetham's School of Music, Manchester, and then at the Royal Northern College of Music. Awards include the Hirsch Prize for Beethoven chamber music and the Century Fund Prize. His freelance commitments include playing as principal cello with the Orchestra of the Swan in Stratford and Mid-Wales Opera, and regular work with the City of Birmingham Symphony Orchestra.

JEREMY BARLOW *harpsichord*
As a performer Jeremy has for many years directed The Broadside Band, playing early wind and keyboard instruments. The group has made more than a

Les interprètes

Le CD accompagnant ce recueil fut enregistré par THE BROADSIDE BAND en janvier 2006 au Trinity College of Music, The Old Royal Naval College, Greenwich, Londres.

Ingénieur du son : Morgan Roberts
Producteur exécutif : Simon Weir
Directeur musical : Jeremy Barlow

L'enregistrement a été réalisé sur un clavecin numérique Roland C-80, fourni par Chamberlain Music (www. chamberlainmusic.com), qui a été enregistré en direct avec les autres interprètes et, simultanément, sur une autre piste pour les plages d'accompagnement.

Les instrumentistes :

SHARON LINDO *violon*
Sharon se produit, enregistre et participe aux tournées de nombreux ensembles de renom spécialisés dans la musique médiévale, renaissance, baroque et folklorique, parmi lesquels The Broadside Band, The Sixteen, The Dufay Collective, Collegium Musicum 90, Sirinu et The New Scorpion Band. Elle dirige le Corelli Orchestra à Cheltenham et a participé aux tournées du Théâtre du Globe de Shakespeare au Japon, en Italie et en Amérique.

JENNIFER STINTON *flûte*
Au cours de ses études, Jenny obtint plusieurs bourses et récompenses à la Royal Academy of Music. Elle signa ensuite un contrat avec Collins Classics et enregistra pour cette maison douze CD recouvrant les grandes œuvres du répertoire de la flûte. En 1991, elle interpréta un concerto pour flûte de Mozart au Royal Festival Hall (Londres) avec le Philharmonia Orchestra, en présence de Diana, princesse de Galles.

NICK STRINGFELLOW *violoncelle*
Nick fit ses études à la Chetham School of Music (Manchester) puis au Royal Northern College of Music. Il fut récompensé par le Hirsch Prize pour la musique de chambre de Beethoven et par le Century Fund Prize. En tant que musicien indépendant, il joue comme premier violoncelle avec l'Orchestra of the Swan à Stratford et avec le Mid-Wales Opera. Il collabore aussi régulièrement avec le City of Birmingham Symphony Orchestra.

JEREMY BARLOW *clavecin*
Interprète des instruments à vent anciens et des claviers, Jeremy dirige The Broadside Band depuis de nombreuses années. Cet ensemble a réalisé plus d'une

Über die Künstler

Die CD, die diesem Heft beiliegt, wurde von THE BROADSIDE BAND im Januar 2006 am Trinity College of Music, The Old Royal Naval College, Greenwich, London, aufgenommen.

Aufnahmetechniker: Morgan Roberts
Leitender Produzent: Simon Weir
Musikdirektor: Jeremy Barlow

Auf der Aufnahme ist ein Roland C-80 Digitalcembalo zu hören, das von Chamberlain Music (www.chamberlainmusic.com) zur Verfügung gestellt wurde. Das Instrument wurde zusammen mit den anderen Musikern akustisch aufgenommen, gleichzeitig aber auch auf einem anderen Kanal für die Mitspielstücke.

Die Instrumentalisten:

SHARON LINDO *Geige*
Sharon gibt Konzerte, macht Aufnahmen und geht mit vielen etablierten Mittelalter-, Renaissance-, Barock- und Volksmusikgruppen, wie z.B. The Broadside Band, The Sixteen, The Dufay Collective, Collegium Musicum 90, Sirinu und The New Scorpion Band auf Konzertreise. Sie leitet das Corelli Orchester in Cheltenham und war mit dem *Shakespeare's Globe* auf Tournee durch Japan, Italien und Amerika.

JENNIFER STINTON *Flöte*
Als Studentin gewann Jennifer mehrere Stipendien und Preise an der Royal Academy of Music. Dann unterschrieb sie einen Vertrag bei Collins Classic und nahm für dieses Label zwölf CDs auf, die die Hauptwerke des Flötenrepertoires abdecken. Im Jahre 1991 spielte sie zusammen mit dem Philharmonia Orchestra ein Flötenkonzert von Mozart in der Royal Festival Hall in London. Bei diesem Konzert war Prinzessin Diana anwesend.

NICK STRINGFELLOW *Cello*
Nick studierte an der Chetham School of Music in Manchester und dann am Royal Northern College of Music. Gewonnene Preise sind z.B. der Hirsch Preis in der Sparte Kammermusik von Beethoven und der Century Fund Prize. Seine freiberuflichen Verpflichtungen umfassen das Spielen des ersten Cellos im Orchestra of the Swan in Stratford und der Mid-Wales Opera, sowie regelmäßige Arbeit mit dem City of Birmingham Symphony Orchestra.

JEREMY BARLOW *Cembalo*
Als Künstler leitete Jeremy viele Jahre lang The Broadside Band, wobei er alte Holzblas- und Tasteninstrumente spielte. Das Ensemble hat mehr als ein Dutzend

dozen CDs, specialising in dance and popular music from the 16th to 18th centuries. His full-scale recording of *The Beggar's Opera* (Hyperion) won an Edison award. For details of his editions and books, see p. 3.

douzaine de CD spécialisés dans la musique de danse et la musique populaire anglaises du XVIe au XVIIIe siècles. Son enregistrement intégral de *The Beggar's Opera* (Hyperion) remporta le prix Edison. (Voir le détail de ses éditions et ouvrages en page 3).

CDs gemacht, wobei es sich auf Tanz- und Unterhaltungsmusik aus dem 16. bis 18. Jahrhundert spezialisiert hat. Seine Kompletteinspielung von *The Beggar's Opera* (Hyperion) gewann den Edison Preis. Nähere Hinweise zu seinen Ausgaben und Büchern, s. S. 3.

CD track list / Plages du CD / CD-Titelverzeichnis

	complete performance	play-along tracks
Marche pour les matelots (Marais)	1	17
Air (Boismortier)	2	18
Rondeau (Boismortier)	3	19
Brunette 'Je suis charmé d'une brune' (Montéclair)	4	20
Gigues 1 & 2 (Corrette)	5	21
Vaudeville (Corrette)	6	22
Le Menuet à 4-6 coupé (Le Clerc)	7	23
La chapelière (Le Clerc)	8	24
Les Grâces et l'enjouement (Le Clerc)	9	25
La chasse galante (Le Clerc)	10	26
Gavotte and Air (Lagarde)	11	27
Branle de Metz (Le Clerc)	12	28
Airs 1 & 2 (Mondonville)	13	29
Contredanses 1 & 2 (Mondonville)	14	30
Air (Mondonville)	15	31
Marche (Mondonville)	16	32
Tuning track (A = 440)	33	